What are bulbs and roots?

by Molly Aloian

🌱 Crabtree Publishing Company

www.crabtreebooks.com

Author
Molly Aloian

Publishing plan research and development
Sean Charlebois, Reagan Miller
Crabtree Publishing Company

Editors
Reagan Miller, Kathy Middleton

Proofreader
Crystal Sikkens

Notes to adults
Reagan Miller

Photo research
Allison Napier, Ken Wright, Crystal Sikkens

Design
Ken Wright

Production coordinator and Prepress technician
Ken Wright

Print coordinator
Katherine Berti

Photographs
Katherin Berti: page 21
Dreamstime: page 19
Thinkstock: title page, pages 4, 6, 12, 13, 14, 15, 18
Other images by Shutterstock and Thinkstock

Library and Archives Canada Cataloguing in Publication

Aloian, Molly
    What are bulbs and roots? / Molly Aloian.

(Plants close-up)
Includes index.
Issued also in electronic formats.
ISBN 978-0-7787-4220-3 (bound).--ISBN 978-0-7787-4225-8 (pbk.)

    1. Roots (Botany)--Juvenile literature. 2. Bulbs (Plant anatomy)--Juvenile literature. 3. Plant anatomy--Juvenile literature. I. Title. II. Series: Plants close-up

QK644.A46 2012   j581.4'98   C2012-900405-7

Library of Congress Cataloging-in-Publication Data

Aloian, Molly.
What are bulbs and roots? / Molly Aloian.
p. cm. -- (Plants close-up)
Includes index.
ISBN 978-0-7787-4220-3 (reinforced library binding : alk. paper) --
ISBN 978-0-7787-4225-8 (pbk. : alk. paper) -- ISBN 978-1-4271-7905-0
(electronic pdf) -- ISBN 978-1-4271-8020-9 (electronic html)
1. Bulbs (Plants)--Juvenile literature. I. Title.

SB425.A46 2012
635.9'1526--dc23

2012001126

Crabtree Publishing Company

www.crabtreebooks.com   1-800-387-7650

Printed in Canada/042012/KR20120316

Published in Canada
Crabtree Publishing
616 Welland Ave.
St. Catharines, Ontario
L2M 5V6

Published in the United States
Crabtree Publishing
PMB 59051
350 Fifth Avenue, 59th Floor
New York, New York 10118

Published in the United Kingdom
Crabtree Publishing
Maritime House
Basin Road North, Hove
BN41 1WR

Published in Australia
Crabtree Publishing
3 Charles Street
Coburg North
VIC 3058

Contents

Plant parts

Plants are living things. They need sunlight, air, water, and nutrients to grow.

All plants have roots, stems, and leaves. Some plants have flowers. Some new plants grow from seeds. Other plants grow from bulbs or roots.

Bulbs

Certain types of plants grow from bulbs instead of seeds. Bulbs are living things, too.

A bulb is made up of short, thick leaves, called **scales**, packed around a fat stem.

scales

stem

Storing food

A bulb is a part of a plant that stores food. The bulb holds just enough food for a new plant to start to grow.

If you split a bulb in half, you will see that it has everything the plant will need to grow— a stem, leaves, and food.

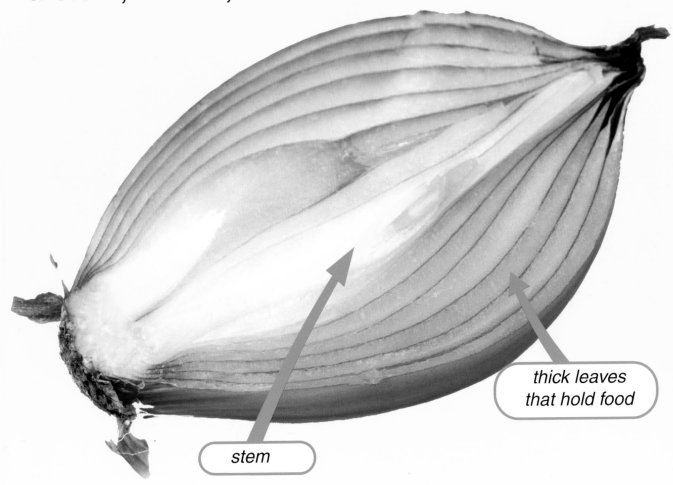

thick leaves that hold food

stem

Is it warm yet?

Bulbs do not grow in winter. They stay buried until the weather gets warmer in spring. A bulb starts to grow a stem and roots when there is rain.

Under the ground, new bulbs grow on the sides of the first bulb. The first bulb is called a **parent plant**. These new bulbs will grow into new plants. A young plant is called a seedling.

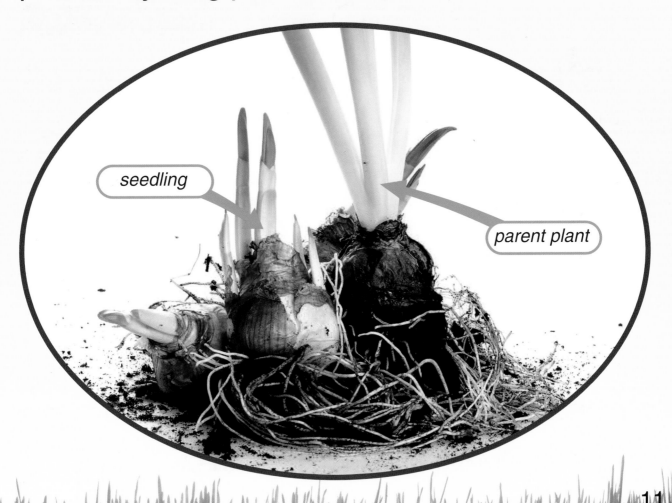

seedling

parent plant

From bulb to flower

A new seedling will stay joined to its parent plant to get the food it needs to grow. The plant can makes its own food when it grows leaves. A flower will also grow on the end of the stem.

Different bulbs grow flowers at different times of the year. Daffodils and tulips have flowers in the spring. Lilies have flowers in the summer.

tulip

New plants from roots

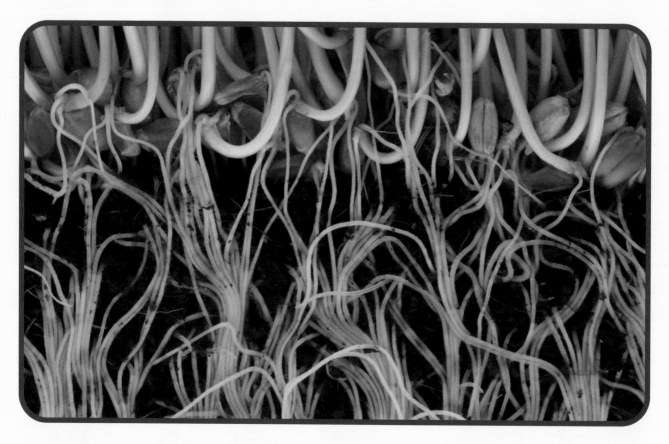

Roots store food, just like bulbs. Roots also hold a plant firmly in soil. They take in water and nutrients.

roots

New plants can also grow from the roots of other plants.

Root parts

Roots have different parts. The primary root is the thickest root. It grows downward. Secondary roots grow from the primary root. They grow sideways.

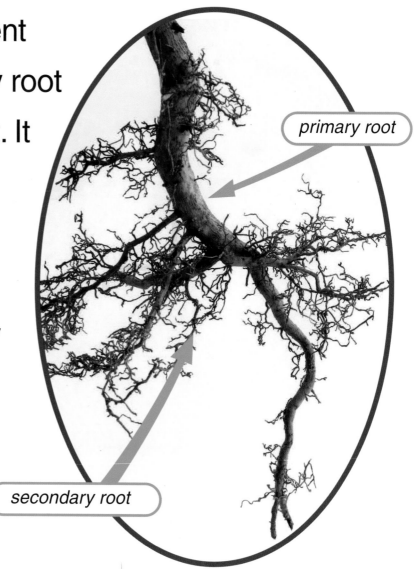

primary root

secondary root

root cap

root hair

Each root has a root cap to protect the tip as it pushes through the soil. Tiny root hairs take in water and nutrients from soil.

Suckers and runners

A chestnut tree can grow from a sucker.

Some plants grow **suckers**. A sucker is a shoot that grows under the ground from a plant's roots. It will grow into a new plant with its own roots.

Strawberries grow from runners.

Some plants grow **runners**. A runner is a shoot that grows above the ground from the bottom of a plant's stem. The runner becomes a new plant with its own roots.

Rhizomes

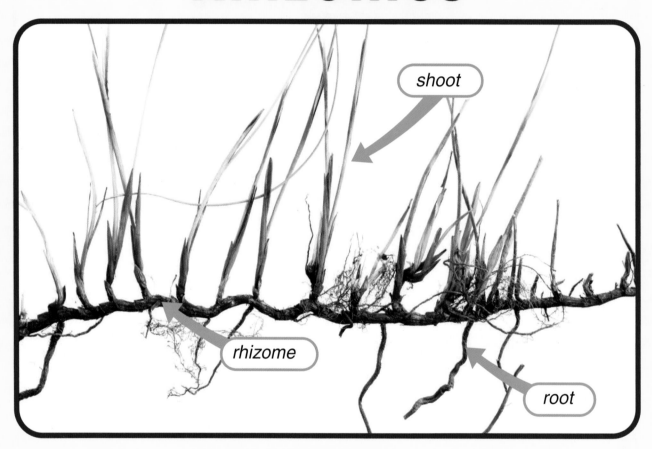

shoot

rhizome

root

Some plants form **rhizomes**. A rhizome is a type of stem that acts like a root. It grows just beneath the surface of the soil beside the parent plant.

New shoots grow out of the rhizome. Iris and calamus plants grow from thick rhizomes.

Good to eat

Bulbs and roots are not food just for plants—they are food for you, too! Roots such as carrots and radishes are good to eat and good for us.

roots

bulbs

Bulbs such as onions and garlic add flavor to our favorite meals.

Words to know

parent plant
11,12

rhizomes 20

runners 19

scales 7

suckers 18

Notes for adults and activities

• Growing from a root

Instructions to adults: Explain that carrots, radishes, and sweet potatoes are examples of roots we eat. Children will experiment with a sweet potato or yam to see if a new plant can grow from the roots of a mature plant. Help children fill a jar with water and insert toothpicks around the top part of the potato. Put the potato in the jar so that the toothpicks rest on top of the jar. Place near a window. Children can record their observations in journals. Both roots and leaves should grow over time.

• Time for tulips!

Instructions to adults: Explain to children that tulips are thought of as a sign of spring. Ask children to discuss how the bulbs, which are planted in fall, survive in winter. What makes them grow in the spring? Give children a tulip bulb to examine its size, texture, color, and other features. Next, examine the inside of a tulip bulb. Ask children how many parts they see and why each part is important.

Learn more

Books

How do plants help us? (My World) by Bobbie Kalman. Crabtree Publishing Company (2011)

Plants are living things (Introducing Living Things) by Bobbie Kalman. Crabtree Publishing Company (2007)

Websites

The Great Plant Escape: Children team up with Detective LePlant to identify plant parts and functions and explore how a plant grows.
http://urbanext.illinois.edu/gpe/index.cfm

Michigan 4-H Children's Garden Tour: This interactive site takes visitors on a virtual garden tour. Children learn about different kinds of plants, play educational games, and answer questions.
http://4hgarden.msu.edu/kidstour/tour.html